I0691150

MAKING EACH
DAY
YOUR BEST

A DAILY PLANNER FOR MEN

ACTIVINOTES

Activinotes

DAILY JOURNALS, PLANNERS, NOTEBOOKS AND OTHER BLANK BOOKS

Copyright 2016

Daily Planner for Men

Date:	

Time:	Activity

Goal for the Day:

Important Activity for the Day:

Reminders for the Day:

Daily Planner for Men

Date:

Time:	Activity

Goal for the Day:

Important Activity for the Day:

Reminders for the Day:

DAILY PLANNER FOR MEN

Date:

Time:	Activity

Goal for the Day:

Important Activity for the Day:

Reminders for the Day:

Daily Planner for Men

Date :

Time:	Activity

Goal for the Day:

Important Activity for the Day:

Reminders for the Day:

Daily Planner for Men

Date:

Time:	Activity

Goal for the Day:

Important Activity for the Day:

Reminders for the Day:

Daily Planner for Men

Date :

Time:	Activity

Goal for the Day:

Important Activity for the Day:

Reminders for the Day:

Daily Planner for Men

Date:

Time:	Activity

Goal for the Day:

Important Activity for the Day:

Reminders for the Day:

Daily Planner for Men

Date :

Time:	Activity

Goal for the Day:

Important Activity for the Day:

Reminders for the Day:

Daily Planner for Men

Date:

Time:	Activity

Goal for the Day:

Important Activity for the Day:

Reminders for the Day:

Daily Planner for Men

Date:

Time:	Activity

Goal for the Day:

Important Activity for the Day:

Reminders for the Day:

Daily Planner for Men

Date:

Time:	Activity

Goal for the Day:

Important Activity for the Day:

Reminders for the Day:

Daily Planner for Men

Date :

Time:	Activity

Goal for the Day:

Important Activity for the Day:

Reminders for the Day:

Daily Planner for Men

Date:

Time:	Activity

Goal for the Day:

Important Activity for the Day:

Reminders for the Day:

Daily Planner for Men

Date:

Time:	Activity

Goal for the Day:

Important Activity for the Day:

Reminders for the Day:

Daily Planner for Men

Date:

Time:	Activity

Goal for the Day:

Important Activity for the Day:

Reminders for the Day:

Daily Planner for Men

Date :	

Time:	Activity

Goal for the Day:

Important Activity for the Day:

Reminders for the Day:

DAILY PLANNER FOR MEN

Date:	

Time:	Activity

Goal for the Day:

Important Activity for the Day:

Reminders for the Day:

Daily Planner for Men

Date:

Time:	Activity

Goal for the Day:

Important Activity for the Day:

Reminders for the Day:

DAILY PLANNER FOR MEN

Date:	

Time:	Activity

Goal for the Day:

Important Activity for the Day:

Reminders for the Day:

Daily Planner for Men

Date :

Time:	Activity

Goal for the Day:

Important Activity for the Day:

Reminders for the Day:

Daily Planner for Men

Date:

Time:	Activity

Goal for the Day:

Important Activity for the Day:

Reminders for the Day:

DaiLY PLanneR FOR MEn

Date:

Time:	Activity

Goal for the Day:

Important Activity for the Day:

Reminders for the Day:

DaiLY PLanneR foR MEn

Date:

Time:	Activity

Goal for the Day:

Important Activity for the Day:

Reminders for the Day:

DAILY PLANNER FOR MEN

Date:

Time:	Activity

Goal for the Day:

Important Activity for the Day:

Reminders for the Day:

Daily Planner for Men

Date:	

Time:	Activity

Goal for the Day:

Important Activity for the Day:

Reminders for the Day:

Daily Planner for Men

Date:

Time:	Activity

Goal for the Day:

Important Activity for the Day:

Reminders for the Day:

Daily Planner for Men

Date:

Time:	Activity

Goal for the Day:

Important Activity for the Day:

Reminders for the Day:

DAILY PLANNER FOR MEN

Date:

Time:	Activity

Goal for the Day:

Important Activity for the Day:

Reminders for the Day:

Daily Planner for Men

Date:

Time:	Activity

Goal for the Day:

Important Activity for the Day:

Reminders for the Day:

DAILY PLANNER FOR MEN

Date:	

Time:	Activity

Goal for the Day:

Important Activity for the Day:

Reminders for the Day:

DAILY PLANNER FOR MEN

Date:

Time:	Activity

Goal for the Day:

Important Activity for the Day:

Reminders for the Day:

Daily Planner for Men

Date:

Time:	Activity

Goal for the Day:

Important Activity for the Day:

Reminders for the Day:

Daily Planner for Men

Date:

Time:	Activity

Goal for the Day:

Important Activity for the Day:

Reminders for the Day:

Daily Planner for Men

Date:	

Time:	Activity

Goal for the Day:

Important Activity for the Day:

Reminders for the Day:

Daily Planner for Men

Date:

Time:	Activity

Goal for the Day:

Important Activity for the Day:

Reminders for the Day:

Daily Planner for Men

Date :	

Time:	Activity

Goal for the Day:

Important Activity for the Day:

Reminders for the Day:

DAILY PLANNER FOR MEN

Date:

Time:	Activity

Goal for the Day:

Important Activity for the Day:

Reminders for the Day:

DAILY PLANNER FOR MEN

Date:

Time:	Activity

Goal for the Day:

Important Activity for the Day:

Reminders for the Day:

DaiLY Planner for Men

Date :

Time:	Activity

Goal for the Day:

Important Activity for the Day:

Reminders for the Day:

Daily Planner for Men

Date :

Time:	Activity

Goal for the Day:

Important Activity for the Day:

Reminders for the Day:

Daily Planner for Men

Date:

Time:	Activity

Goal for the Day:

Important Activity for the Day:

Reminders for the Day:

DAILY PLANNER FOR MEN

Date:	

Time:	Activity

Goal for the Day:

Important Activity for the Day:

Reminders for the Day:

Daily Planner for Men

Date:	

Time:	Activity

Goal for the Day:

Important Activity for the Day:

Reminders for the Day:

Daily Planner for Men

Date:

Time:	Activity

Goal for the Day:

Important Activity for the Day:

Reminders for the Day:

Daily Planner for Men

Date:

Time:	Activity

Goal for the Day:

Important Activity for the Day:

Reminders for the Day:

DAILY PLANNER FOR MEN

Date :

Time:	Activity

Goal for the Day:

Important Activity for the Day:

Reminders for the Day:

Daily Planner for Men

Date:

Time:	Activity

Goal for the Day:

Important Activity for the Day:

Reminders for the Day:

DAILY PLANNER FOR MEN

Date :

Time:	Activity

Goal for the Day:

Important Activity for the Day:

Reminders for the Day:

DAILY PLANNER FOR MEN

Date:

Time:	Activity

Goal for the Day:

Important Activity for the Day:

Reminders for the Day:

Daily Planner for Men

Date:

Time:	Activity

Goal for the Day:

Important Activity for the Day:

Reminders for the Day:

Daily Planner for Men

Date :

Time:	Activity

Goal for the Day:

Important Activity for the Day:

Reminders for the Day:

Daily Planner for Men

Date :	

Time:	Activity

Goal for the Day:

Important Activity for the Day:

Reminders for the Day:

DAILY PLANNER FOR MEN

Date:

Time:	Activity

Goal for the Day:

Important Activity for the Day:

Reminders for the Day:

Daily Planner for Men

Date :

Time:	Activity

Goal for the Day:

Important Activity for the Day:

Reminders for the Day:

Daily Planner for Men

Date:

Time:	Activity

Goal for the Day:

Important Activity for the Day:

Reminders for the Day:

Daily Planner for Men

Date:	

Time:	Activity

Goal for the Day:

Important Activity for the Day:

Reminders for the Day:

Daily Planner for Men

Date:

Time:	Activity

Goal for the Day:

Important Activity for the Day:

Reminders for the Day:

DAILY PLANNER FOR MEN

Date:

Time:	Activity

Goal for the Day:

Important Activity for the Day:

Reminders for the Day:

Daily Planner for Men

Date:

Time:	Activity

Goal for the Day:

Important Activity for the Day:

Reminders for the Day:

Daily Planner for Men

Date :	

Time:	Activity

Goal for the Day:

Important Activity for the Day:

Reminders for the Day:

DAILY PLANNER FOR MEN

Date:

Time:	Activity

Goal for the Day:

Important Activity for the Day:

Reminders for the Day:

Daily Planner for Men

Date:

Time:	Activity

Goal for the Day:

Important Activity for the Day:

Reminders for the Day:

DAILY PLANNER FOR MEN

Date:

Time:	Activity

Goal for the Day:

Important Activity for the Day:

Reminders for the Day:

DAILY PLANNER FOR MEN

Date :	

Time:	Activity

Goal for the Day:

Important Activity for the Day:

Reminders for the Day:

Daily Planner for Men

Date:

Time:	Activity

Goal for the Day:

Important Activity for the Day:

Reminders for the Day:

DAILY PLANNER FOR MEN

Date:	

Time:	Activity

Goal for the Day:

Important Activity for the Day:

Reminders for the Day:

Daily Planner for Men

Date:

Time:	Activity

Goal for the Day:

Important Activity for the Day:

Reminders for the Day:

Daily Planner for Men

Date:

Time:	Activity

Goal for the Day:

Important Activity for the Day:

Reminders for the Day:

Daily Planner for Men

Date:

Time:	Activity

Goal for the Day:

Important Activity for the Day:

Reminders for the Day:

DAILY PLANNER FOR MEN

Date:	

Time:	Activity

Goal for the Day:

Important Activity for the Day:

Reminders for the Day:

Daily Planner for Men

Date :

Time:	Activity

Goal for the Day:

Important Activity for the Day:

Reminders for the Day:

Daily Planner for Men

Date:

Time:	Activity

Goal for the Day:

Important Activity for the Day:

Reminders for the Day:

Daily Planner for Men

Date:

Time:	Activity

Goal for the Day:

Important Activity for the Day:

Reminders for the Day:

DAILY PLANNER FOR MEN

Date:

Time:	Activity

Goal for the Day:

Important Activity for the Day:

Reminders for the Day:

Daily Planner for Men

Date:	

Time:	Activity

Goal for the Day:

Important Activity for the Day:

Reminders for the Day:

Daily Planner for Men

Date:	

Time:	Activity

Goal for the Day:

Important Activity for the Day:

Reminders for the Day:

DAILY PLANNER FOR MEN

Date:

Time:	Activity

Goal for the Day:

Important Activity for the Day:

Reminders for the Day:

Daily Planner for Men

Date:

Time:	Activity

Goal for the Day:

Important Activity for the Day:

Reminders for the Day:

Daily Planner for Men

Date:

Time:	Activity

Goal for the Day:

Important Activity for the Day:

Reminders for the Day:

Daily Planner for Men

Date :

Time:	Activity

Goal for the Day:

Important Activity for the Day:

Reminders for the Day:

DAILY PLANNER FOR MEN

Date:	

Time:	Activity

Goal for the Day:

Important Activity for the Day:

Reminders for the Day:

DAILY PLANNER FOR MEN

Date :

Time:	Activity

Goal for the Day:

Important Activity for the Day:

Reminders for the Day:

Daily Planner for Men

Date:	

Time:	Activity

Goal for the Day:

Important Activity for the Day:

Reminders for the Day:

DAILY PLANNER FOR MEN

Date:	

Time:	Activity

Goal for the Day:

Important Activity for the Day:

Reminders for the Day:

DAILY PLANNER FOR MEN

Date:

Time:	Activity

Goal for the Day:

Important Activity for the Day:

Reminders for the Day:

Daily Planner for Men

Date:

Time:	Activity

Goal for the Day:

Important Activity for the Day:

Reminders for the Day:

Daily Planner for Men

Date:	

Time:	Activity

Goal for the Day:

Important Activity for the Day:

Reminders for the Day:

Daily Planner for Men

Date:	

Time:	Activity

Goal for the Day:

Important Activity for the Day:

Reminders for the Day:

Daily Planner for Men

Date:

Time:	Activity

Goal for the Day:

Important Activity for the Day:

Reminders for the Day:

Daily Planner for Men

Date :

Time:	Activity

Goal for the Day:

Important Activity for the Day:

Reminders for the Day:

Daily Planner for Men

Date:

Time:	Activity

Goal for the Day:

Important Activity for the Day:

Reminders for the Day:

DAILY PLANNER FOR MEN

Date:	

Time:	Activity

Goal for the Day:

Important Activity for the Day:

Reminders for the Day:

Daily Planner for Men

Date:

Time:	Activity

Goal for the Day:

Important Activity for the Day:

Reminders for the Day:

Daily Planner for Men

Date:

Time:	Activity

Goal for the Day:

Important Activity for the Day:

Reminders for the Day:

Daily Planner for Men

Date:

Time:	Activity

Goal for the Day:

Important Activity for the Day:

Reminders for the Day:

DAILY PLANNER FOR MEN

Date :	

Time:	Activity

Goal for the Day:

Important Activity for the Day:

Reminders for the Day:

Daily Planner for Men

Date:	

Time:	Activity

Goal for the Day:

Important Activity for the Day:

Reminders for the Day:

DAILY PLANNER FOR MEN

Date:	

Time:	Activity

Goal for the Day:

Important Activity for the Day:

Reminders for the Day:

DAILY PLANNER FOR MEN

Date:	

Time:	Activity

Goal for the Day:

Important Activity for the Day:

Reminders for the Day:

Daily Planner for Men

Date:

Time:	Activity

Goal for the Day:

Important Activity for the Day:

Reminders for the Day:

Daily Planner for Men

Date:	

Time:	Activity

Goal for the Day:

Important Activity for the Day:

Reminders for the Day:

Daily Planner for Men

Date :

Time:	Activity

Goal for the Day:

Important Activity for the Day:

Reminders for the Day:

Daily Planner for Men

Date:	

Time:	Activity

Goal for the Day:

Important Activity for the Day:

Reminders for the Day:

Daily Planner for Men

Date :

Time:	Activity

Goal for the Day:

Important Activity for the Day:

Reminders for the Day: